New Ideas in GLASS PAINTING

New Ideas in GLASS PAINTING

Katherine Duncan Aimone

LARK BOOKS

A Division of Sterling Publishing Co., Inc.
New York

ART DIRECTOR: Thom Gaines

PHOTOGRAPHY: Keith Wright (www.keithwright.com)

ILLUSTRATIONS: Orrin Lundgren

EDITORIAL ASSISTANCE: Rain Newcomb, Veronika Alice Gunter

COVER DESIGN: Barbara Zaretsky

Library of Congress Cataloging-in-Publication Data
Duncan-Aimone, Katherine.
        New ideas in glass painting / by Katherine Duncan Aimone.
                p. cm.
        Includes index.
        ISBN 1-57990-287-1 (pbk.)
        1. Glass painting and staining—Technique. I. Title.

        TT298 .D863 2002
        748.5'028'2—dc21   2001041404
                                                        CIP

10 9 8 7 6 5 4 3 2 1
First Edition

Published by Lark Books, a division of
Sterling Publishing Co., Inc.
387 Park Avenue South, New York, N.Y. 10016

©2002, Lark Books

 Distributed in Canada by Sterling Publishing,
c/o Canadian Manda Group, One Atlantic Ave., Suite 105
Toronto, Ontario, Canada M6K 3E7

Distributed in the U.K. by:
Guild of Master Craftsman Publications Ltd.
Castle Place, 166 High Street, Lewes East Sussex, England BN7 1XU
Tel: (+ 44) 1273 477374, Fax: (+ 44) 1273 478606,
Email: pubs@thegmcgroup.com, Web: www.gmcpublications.com

 Distributed in Australia by Capricorn Link (Australia) Pty Ltd., P.O. Box 704,
Windsor, NSW 2756 Australia

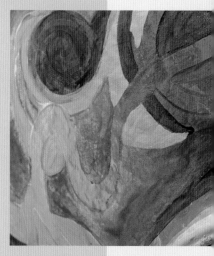

The written instructions, photographs, designs, patterns, and projects in this volume are intended for the personal use of the reader and may be reproduced for that purpose only. Any other use, especially commercial use, is forbidden under law without written permission of the copyright holder.

Every effort has been made to ensure that all the information in this book is accurate. However, due to differing conditions, tools, and individual skills, the publisher cannot be responsible for any injuries, losses, and other damages that may result from the use of the information in this book.

 If you have questions or comments about this book, please contact:
Lark Books
67 Broadway
Asheville, NC 28801
(828) 236-9730

Printed in China

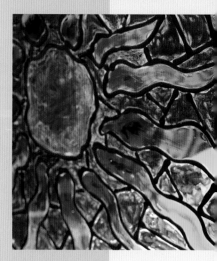

 ISBN 1-57990-287-1

Table of Contents

Introduction

Today, the popular craft of painting on glass is more accessible and diverse than ever. Look around and you'll see evidence of this widespread trend everywhere—from department store shelves to the windows of chic boutiques and home decor stores.

Why not paint your own glass masterpieces rather than buy them? This book explores some of the newest glass painting ideas through projects that will open your eyes to a world of creative possibilities. Whether you paint simple square votives in bright colors for a backyard soirée or embellish a statuesque vase for your dining room table, you'll find that painting glass will satisfy both your creative and practical sides.

You'll be amazed at how simple this art is once you learn a few basic techniques and tricks of the trade that can be applied in many different ways. And today's glass paints come in a dazzling array of colors and finishes that are simple to clean up with soap and water.

So, turn the page to learn about paints, tools, and techniques before lingering for a while over 40 engaging projects that range from wineglasses to tabletops. Then, choose a favorite one or two, collect some paints and brushes, and you'll be ready to begin.

Only one caveat is in order as you embark on this wonderful journey—painting glass can be addictive!

the Basics: TOOLS, MATERIALS, TECHNIQUES

Glass Paints

Glass paints come in different forms and an array of colors. Some are packaged in bottles, some in tubes. Some are set by allowing them to air-dry for a length of time, and others are made to be heat-set in a conventional oven. Spray-on glass paints that produce even surface coverage are also available.

Glass is nonporous, so you need to clean the surface thoroughly to remove grease, fingerprints, and smudges, or the paint may not adhere properly. You should always clean it by washing it with mild detergent and water or with glass cleaner (vinegar mixed with water works well). To further clean the glass, you can use rubbing alcohol or surface conditioner (if recommended by the paint manufacturer). Some paints claim that the paint will be less likely to peel off if the glass is first treated with their brand of surface conditioner, which acts as a bonding agent between the glass and the paint.

Most glass paints are water-based and clean up easily with water. Always stir or shake them before using them, and remove excess water from paintbrushes before painting with them. (Too much water in the brush can dilute the paint.) Keep a jar with water handy as well as a some paper towels to clean your brushes while you work. And, for that occasional slip of the brush, you can use a moistened cotton swab to lift the paint off the surface.

AIR-DRY AND HEAT-SET PAINTS

Air-dry paints are easy to use, but they require a specified length of time to dry and cure to prevent them from peeling or flaking off the surface (sometimes as long as 10 days). Always read the instructions on your particular paint or you may end up with your work going down the drain (literally)! Another caveat related to this subject: you should note the drying time between coats that the manufacturer recommends to make sure that your paint remains intact.

Heat-set paints are also simple to use, and some designers prefer them for functional, everyday glassware that will be washed over and over (such as glasses, plates, and bowls). Once these paints dry on the glassware, the pieces are placed in a preheated oven set at around 300°F (150°C) for about 30 minutes. (Again, always read the instructions on your specific paint for times.) After following the paint manufacturer's instructions for either drying or heat-setting the

Before painting, always clean the glass by washing it in mild detergent and water or with glass cleaner (a mixture of vinegar and water works well). If your paint recommends applying surface conditioner after cleaning the glass, make sure to take this extra step.

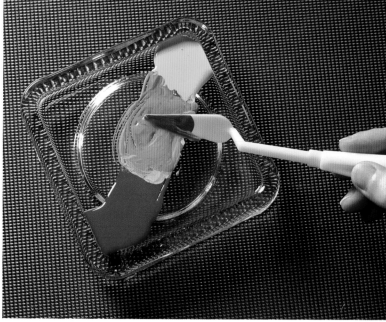

Blending together red and yellow paints to make orange.

paint, most paints are microwave and ovensafe up to 350°F (194°C).

Neither air-dry nor heat-set water-based paints are foodsafe. (In other words, it isn't a great idea to put food or your lips directly on the paint.) This is easy enough to solve if you simply leave an unpainted band at the top of all glasses, and paint on the back of plates or bowls instead of the front. Nevertheless, use common sense with these matters—you're not going to keel over if you eat a cookie that has touched a painted glass surface!

Some paints suggest that you use a top coat after allowing the colors to dry as a kind of glaze to seal the surface. This is not a necessary step, but if you like a more smooth, finished look, you might prefer the addition of this clear coat. And, it only makes sense that an extra layer on top of the paint could help to protect the paint from scratches. Top coats come in a variety of finishes: matte, satin, gloss, and even frosted! (Adding a top coat is an option for any project you undertake in this book, even though we haven't listed it in the materials lists.)

Paint Tips:

- Check the paint manufacturer's color chart at the point of purchase because paint often looks different in the bottle than in finished form (for example, frosted colors appear glossy in the bottle, but dry to a frosted, matte finish).

- ALWAYS read the instructions on your particular brand of paint because they vary.

- Before you choose to buy a lot of a paint, test it out to see how you like it. Some people prefer the look and feel of air-dry paints, others like the idea of firing the paint in an oven.

- Practice painting on junk glass from the recycling bin.

- Don't use air-dry and heat-set paints together on the same piece.

- If you blend paints together, blend ones from the same line made by the same manufacturer.

- Use a color wheel to figure out which colors blend to make new ones.

PAINT FINISHES

Glass paints are generally available in opaque or transparent/translucent forms. The transparent paints are often used to create a stained-glass effect, and the opaque paints give solid coverage. Glass paints also come in other finishes such as pearlized, frosted, etched effect, and satin.

GEL/TEXTURED PAINTS

Glass paints are available in water-based gel form, which can be squeezed directly from the tube onto the glass to create a raised effect. If you don't want a textured surface, you can shake or stir it to liquify it before brushing it on. After gel paints dry, they are translucent.

LINER PAINT

These paints come in tubes and bottles equipped with tips for squeezing the paint into consistent lines. They're available in a wide variety of colors and are used to draw outlines or other lines. This paint is called liquid leading when it is used to simulate lead in faux stained-glass designs. Moving slowly with the liner tip renders a wider line; moving quickly thins it.

SPRAY GLASS PAINTS

Spray-on glass paints provide extremely even coverage on the surface of glass. They can be used to cover a whole piece of glass with one color, layered to create new colors, or sprayed in overlapping bands to create a rainbowlike effect. Areas of the glass can be masked with

Glass paints are available in opaque and transparent forms.

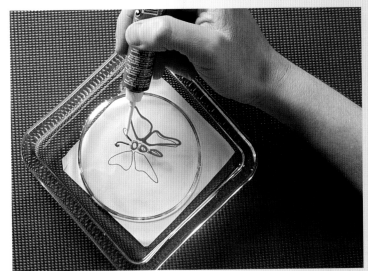
You can squeeze out distinct outlines with liner paints.

tape or vinyl to create clean designs on a piece (see project on page 62). If you use this type of paint, always read the directions and precautions before using it. Use it in a well-ventilated room, or, preferably, outside. The fumes can be harmful to breathe.

OTHER PAINTS

Glass painters adapt other paints to glass, such as artist's acrylic paints or latex paints. These paints should not be used on items that will be washed, but can be used on decorative items. Paint pens, available at craft stores, can also be used on decorative glass pieces.

Applying the Paint

Glass paint is applied with the same tools as other paints: brushes, sponges, stamps, and so forth. You can be as traditional or as inventive as you like with this medium—from painting with a brush to stamping with a piece of window screen.

BRUSHES

Becoming familiar with artist's brushes and trying them out is fundamental to your success with glass painting. Brushes come in all shapes, sizes, and degrees of stiffness. The size of the bristles changes the look of the mark they make. Some are measured by width, others by numbers: the lower the number, the finer the brush. They range widely in cost, depending in part on whether they are made of natural or synthetic bristles. Any brush that creates an effect that you like shouldn't be overlooked.

Brushes come in a variety of sizes and several shapes. Sponge-tipped applicator brushes can be used to apply paint to large areas. Load your brush with paint from a plastic palette, or improvise by using a home item such as an old ceramic plate.

Use common sense to choose brushes by thinking about what kind of marks they'll make. Investigate brushes at art and craft supply stores and even hardware stores. Pick them up and pluck them to test how hard or soft the bristles are. Experiment and find the ones that are the most comfortable to use.

Test them out on throwaway pieces of glass to see the kinds of brushstrokes they make. Experiment with line widths. For example, moving the brush quickly will produce a thinner line, while moving it slowly will produce a thicker line. Use a fine-pointed round brush (what we refer to in the projects as a "liner brush") for painting outlines and a flat, wide brush for filling in large areas of color.

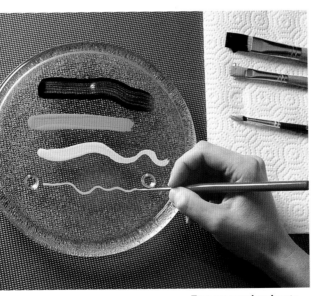

Test out your brushes to see what kinds of brushstrokes they produce.

Sponges can be used to apply paint in inventive ways, masking tape and self-adhesive vinyl can be cut to produce stencils, and rubber stamps as well as common found materials can be used to stamp paint on glass.

SPONGES

Sponges loaded with glass paint can be used to fill in backgrounds, print shapes, or color an entire piece of glass. From the common kitchen sponge to natural sea sponges, you can use different sponges to create various effects.

Compacted sponges, such as wedge cosmetic sponges, will provide smooth, even coverage with a couple of coats of paint, while larger-pored sponges, such as kitchen sponges, will create a textured surface.

Flat sponges can be cut into shapes to print on your glass, or you can purchase precut shapes at craft stores to use as stamps. Small sponges are handy for

Compact wedge sponges produce smooth painted effects, while larger-pored sponges produce a mottled effect.

Cut a flat sponge into a shape, and use it as a stamp.

Cut shapes from vinyl to make both positive and negative stencils. (This piece was sprayed with glass paint before removing the stencil.)

Vinyl leading can be used to form a natural border for painted areas.

stencilling. Sponge-tipped applicator brushes can be used to brush in larger areas.

MASKING SUPPLIES

Common masking tape can be used to cover parts of the glass surface before painting. After the paint dries, the tape is removed to reveal a stripe or simple shape on the glass. For more detailed shapes, self-adhesive vinyl can be cut with scissors and adhered to the glass to mask it from paint. Both positive and negative stencils can be created with vinyl.

SELF-STICK LEADING

Faux leading made of vinyl strips can be used on decorative glass pieces to create a mosaiclike effect. Cut the strips to size, and stick them on the glass to form borders where you want them before filling in the areas with paint.

STAMPS

Rubber stamps or hand-carved stamps can be used to apply glass paint. You can apply paint to larger stamps with an artist's brayer (a tool with a rubber roller attached to it), or press the stamp into paint that you've spread onto your palette with a sponge or brush. Because the glass surface is slick, you may have some trouble getting a crisp image with a stamp. If you do, experiment to find the paint thickness needed to press a clean image. Try removing excess paint by lightly patting the loaded stamp on a paper towel before pressing it to the glass.

If you use textured items to print with, such as leaves or pieces of window screen, place the items on old newspaper and sponge or

You can use found items such as leaves or window screen to print textured shapes and backgrounds on glass.

Trace an image on glass with a pen and a piece of transfer paper.

brush them with paint to saturate the surface. Use a clean sponge to lightly dab excess paint from the item to reveal the texture. (Doing this will help to prevent making a smeary image on the glass.) Pull the textured item away from the newspaper, and press it lightly onto the glass. Use a clean sponge to press the item firmly into place before peeling it up to reveal the stamped image.

DESIGN TEMPLATES

The easiest way to paint an image on a piece of glass is to tape a drawn or photocopied version of it underneath the area that you intend to paint. You can also trace the image onto the glass using a pen and a piece of transfer paper. Place the transfer paper between the image and glass, then tape it into place. The back of this book has templates included that you can enlarge to use in this way, but you can also draw your own templates, or use copyright-free images as templates.

Once you've sized your image, you can outline it by holding it in place underneath the glass with masking tape. Loosely paint in the shapes of the image with color, allow them to dry slightly, and outline them with liner paint if you wish.

CLEANUP TOOLS

During the process of painting glass, you can wipe away mistakes with moistened cotton swabs while the paint is still wet, or wipe off large areas of paint with a moistened paper towel. If you want to change something after the paint has already dried, you can scrape it away with a single- edged razor blade or the sharp edge of a craft knife. If you find that you don't like the whole design that you've created with water-based paint, and the paint's been dry only for a few hours or less, try running water over the paint and scrubbing it until the paint flakes and peels off. Then you can start over!

Clean up mistakes in wet paint with moistened cotton swabs or paper towels. After the paint is dry, you can scrape off mistakes with a single-edged razor blade or the edge of a craft knife.

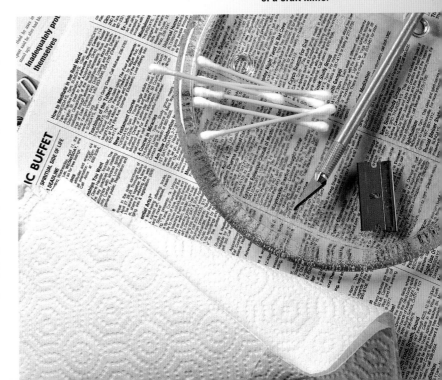

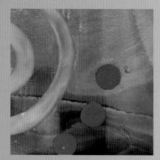
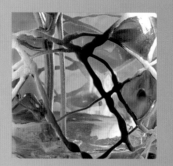

The Projects

From the simplest ideas to the most complex, the following pages will provide you with enough inspiration to keep the paint flowing for many satisfying hours.

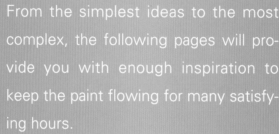

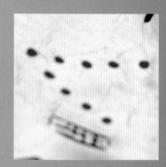

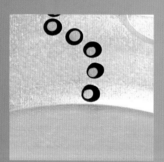
Use these ideas exactly as they are or as a springboard for your own variations. Settle in to your work space, relax, and enjoy experimenting—once your imagination is sparked, you'll lose yourself in the creative process.

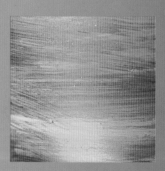

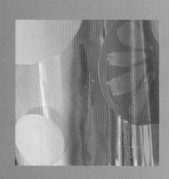

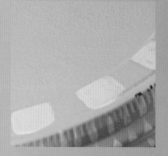
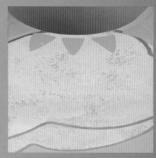

Easy Votives

Square glass votives can be painted with any combination of colors to create small, jewel-like luminaries that brighten up a party or summer night on the patio.

MATERIALS *and* TOOLS

- **2 square glass votives**
- **Mild detergent**
- **Surface conditioner (if recommended by the paint manufacturer)**
- **Frosted glass paints: yellow, orange, blue, green**
- **Medium flat brush**
- **Glass paint liners in bottles or tubes: gold, black**
- **2 votive candles**

INSTRUCTIONS

1. Wash and dry the votives. Apply surface conditioner if recommended for use with your paints.

2. Paint the four sides of each votive with one of the frosted paints. Paint the top rim as well.

3. Allow the first coat of paint to dry, then add a second coat. (If you're using a dark color, you may want to skip painting one side of the votive with a second coat so that the candle will show.)

4. After the second coat dries, paint the bottoms of the votives with contrasting colors, and allow the paint to dry.

5. Flip the votives over, and squeeze a line of dots in black or gold on the top of the flat rim.

6. Follow the paint manufacturer's instructions for either drying or baking the paint.

7. Place candles in the votives.

DESIGNER: Katherine Aimone

Showy Water Glasses

Bands of bright color in the center of these glasses are poised atop the firm footing of square bases outlined in color.

INSTRUCTIONS

1 Wash and dry the glasses. Apply surface conditioner if recommended for use with your paints.

2 Pull off about 2 inches (5.1 cm) of masking tape, and tape it to the top of one of the glasses along the edge. Add another strip of tape down the center of the glass so that the two pieces form a "T".

3 Add two more pieces of tape on either side of the central piece of tape.

4 Remove the central piece of tape to reveal a masked strip down the center of the glass. Add a short piece of tape at the bottom of the central strip just above the stem of the glass.

5 Repeat the previous steps to add tape frames to the remaining glasses.

6 Squeeze out small portions of the paints on your palette or plate.

7 Within these taped frames, paint combinations of blue and pink paint or orange and purple paint in random horizontal stripes.

8 Allow the paint to dry slightly, then use the other end of your paint brush to scratch looping and curling lines in the paint.

9 Allow the paint to dry slightly, then pull away the tape strips to reveal a rough edge around the painted strips.

10 Paint the edges of each of the bases of the glasses with a coordinating color. Apply two coats if needed for coverage.

11 Follow the paint manufacturer's instructions for either drying or baking the paint.

DESIGNER: Katherine Aimone

MATERIALS and TOOLS

- **4 round beverage glasses with square bases**
- **Mild detergent**
- **Surface conditioner (if recommended by the paint manufacturer)**
- **¾-inch-wide (1.9 cm) masking tape**
- **Artist's palette or old ceramic plate**
- **Opaque glass paints: hot pink, bright blue, bright orange, and purple**
- **Medium flat brush**

Pollock's Bowls

In homage to Abstract Expressionist painter Jackson Pollock, drip and pour your way to an improvisationally designed set of bowls that are as unique as your own signature.

MATERIALS *and* TOOLS

- **3 glass nesting bowls**
- **Mild detergent**
- **Surface conditioner (if recommended by the paint manufacturer)**
- **Masking tape**
- **Old newspapers**
- **Several applicator bottles with squeeze tips (available at craft stores)**
- **Opaque glass paints: black, white, and violet**
- **Craft knife**

INSTRUCTIONS

1. Wash and dry the bowls. Apply surface conditioner if recommended for use with your glass paints.

2. Cover the top edges of the bowls with a ½-inch (1.3 cm) ring of masking tape.

3. Cover a large space on your work area floor with newspapers.

4. Fill each of the applicator bottles with a different color of paint.

5. Turn the bowls upside down on the floor in a row on the newspapers.

6. Stand above the bowls and begin by holding the black paint bottle upside down a couple of feet above the bowls.

7. Squeeze the bottle so that the paint squirts out, and arc the paint back and forth in random lines on the bowls, allowing it to spill onto the newspapers.

(Don't overdo the use of black. You still have several more colors with which to work.) Allow the paint to dry slightly.

8. Add white and violet lines in the same fashion, developing a rhythm for your lines as you go. To make wider lines, slow down the movement of your hand; to make thinner line, move your hand in a quicker motion. (Be careful not to layer too much paint onto the bowls or it may begin to crack and will take too long to dry.) Allow the paint to dry thoroughly.

9. Use the craft knife to cut along the edge of the masking tape that meets the paint. Remove the masking tape to reveal a clean lip. Scrape off any excess paint with the knife.

10. Follow the paint manufacturer's instructions for either drying or baking the paint.

DESIGNER: Diana Light

Painted and Draped Colored Bottles

Finding the most interesting bottles that you can is the first and most important step in this project. Then add your own decorative touches of painted spirals and draped beads (anything goes!). Follow our color scheme, or invent your own to accommodate the bottles that you find.

MATERIALS
and TOOLS

- **3 oversized decorative bottles with stoppers (we chose blue, green, and clear bottles)**

- **Mild detergent**

- **Surface conditioner (if recommended by the paint manufacturer)**

- **Frosted paints: opaque blue, green, orange**

- **Artist's palette or old ceramic plate**

- **Medium round brush with good point**

- **Plastic beaded bracelet sets strung on elastic (made for children and teens, available at some mall clothing stores and in the children's section of general stores)**

- **Charms or dangles (optional)**

- **Jump rings (optional)**

- **Needle-nose pliers (optional)**

INSTRUCTIONS

1 Wash and dry the bottles. Apply surface conditioner if recommended for use with your paint.

2 Squeeze out small portions of the frosted paints onto the artist's palette or plate.

3 Paint large blue spirals or other simple abstract designs on the fronts of any of your bottles that have flat or slightly curved sides. Accent the spirals with dots of orange paint.

4 On round bottles, paint horizontal accent stripes in blue, green, and orange to highlight the shape of the bottle (for instance, our round bottle has rows of curved ripples on its surface that served as a wonderful excuse to add painted stripes).

5 Follow the paint manufacturer's instructions for either drying or baking the paint.

6 Loop and drape colored bracelet sets around the necks of the bottles until you like the way they look.

7 If you want to add a charm or dangle to your bracelet, use the needle-nose pliers to help open the ring at the slit by pulling one part of it up and away from the other to allow room for sliding on a charm or dangle. (Avoid pulling the ring out and apart at the slit, or it may break.)

8 Slide jump rings onto the strings of beads, and add charms or dangles before closing the rings with the pliers.

DESIGNER: Diana Light

Festive Glasses and Plate

Dancing triangles and spirals placed in random, overlapping patterns adorn the rim of this platter. Add simple triangles and spirals to the front of wineglasses, and your guests will be certain to raise them in a toast to you!

INSTRUCTIONS

1 Wash and dry the glassware. Apply surface conditioner to the back of the plate and the glasses if recommended for use with your paint.

2 Turn the plate over on your work surface. Use the gold glass liner to squeeze out a series of spirals around the rim of the plate, improvising as you go. Allow the paint to dry.

3 Squeeze a dollop of each of the frosted paints onto your palette or plate. Load the triangular side of one of the sponges with one of the paint colors.

4 Grasp the sponge by its dry side, and firmly press the sponge inside the rim of the plate's rim on top of the gold design. Pull the sponge off to reveal a triangular print. To increase the opacity of the print, allow the paint to dry slightly, and add a second sponging.

5 Randomly sponge triangular prints around the rim with the three colors. (Use a different sponge for each color.)

Overlap the triangles, and mix colors as you like.

6 Use the opaque glass liners to squeeze accent lines around the triangles and dots between them, keeping in mind that the lines will show through the front only if you squeeze them onto unpainted areas.

7 Use one of the paint colors to sponge a triangular shape on the front of one of the glasses. Allow the paint to dry.

8 Use the gold liner to squeeze a spiral shape on top of the triangle.

9 Add a similar design in another color to the other glass.

10 Squeeze a line of white dots around the rims of the glasses with the white glass liner. (Hold the bottle perpendicular to the base of the glass, squeeze lightly, and quickly remove the bottle to reveal a dot.)

11 Follow the paint manufacturer's instructions for either drying or baking the paint.

DESIGNER: Katherine Aimone

MATERIALS *and* TOOLS

- **12-inch (30.5 cm) glass platter**
- **2 wineglasses**
- **Mild detergent**
- **Surface conditioner (if recommended by the paint manufacturer)**
- **Opaque glass liner: gold, white, black**
- **Frosted glass paints: hot pink, turquoise, indigo blue**
- **Artist's palette or old ceramic plate**
- **Wedge cosmetic sponges**

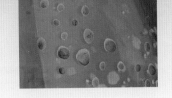

Effervescent Candle Holder

Tiny bubbles float up the sides of this curvaceous candle holder, providing a playful silhouette for candlelight.

27

MATERIALS and TOOLS

- **Tall hurricane-style candle holder**
- **Mild detergent**
- **Surface conditioner (if recommended by the paint manufacturer)**
- **Glass liner paint in squeeze bottles: silver, gold**
- **2 thick books**

INSTRUCTIONS

1. Wash and dry the candleholder. Apply surface conditioner if recommended for use with your paint.

2. Begin decorating the holder by squeezing out a wavy line of gold paint all the way around the foot about ½-inch (1.3 cm) from the edge. Allow the paint to dry, then paint a second line in silver that weaves in and out of the gold line.

3. Repeat this interlocking line motif around the neck of the holder.

4. Squeeze small, randomly placed dots of gold and silver paint onto the foot of the holder. (To do this, hold the squeeze bottle upside down, squeeze, and lightly touch the tip of the bottle to the glass before removing it quickly.) Allow the paint to dry.

5. Roll the holder over on its side, and place a thick book on either side of it to anchor it. Squeeze out a pattern of gold and silver dots of various sizes that move up the side of the holder like floating bubbles. Allow the paint to dry thoroughly.

6. Roll the holder over to expose the unpainted side, and add another pattern of dots that drift upward. Allow the paint to dry.

7. Turn the holder upright, and turn it while you add other random dots between these streams to create a spontaneous effect.

8. Follow the paint manufacturer's instructions for either drying or baking the paint.

DESIGNER: Tana Boerger

Mardi Gras Plate and Glass

This shimmering metallic plate and matching glass

will make an ordinary day worth celebrating.

INSTRUCTIONS
for PLATE

1 Wash and dry the plate and glass. Apply surface conditioner if recommended for use with your paint.

2 Cut the piece of white paper into a circle that is the same size as the center of the plate (excluding the rim). Flip the plate over onto your work surface, and place the paper on the back of the plate to mask it while you paint the rim.

3 Use scissors to snip off the tip of the black paint container so that you'll be able to draw a somewhat thick line (the further down the tip you go, the thicker the line will be). Repeat this process with the gold paint.

4 Use scissors to snip off the tip of the copper paint container close to the top so that you can squeeze out a thin line.

5 Using the finished photo as a guide, draw two intertwining squiggly lines with the copper liner down one side of the plate and on either side of the rim.

6 Draw thin single gold lines on either side of the rim with the gold paint, followed by thicker black lines.

7 Squeeze on a line of small gold dots that run from one side of the rim to the other. Allow the paint to dry.

8 Squeeze out portions of the silver and black paint on the artist's palette. Use the eraser end of the pencil to stamp black dots behind the gold dots. Allow the paint to dry.

9 Remove the paper mask, and use the thick brush to paint over the entire plate with a thick coat of silver paint.

10 Follow the paint manufacturer's instructions for either drying or baking the paint.

INSTRUCTIONS
for WINE GLASS

1 Dab the eraser end of the pencil in black paint, and create a curving line of black dots that runs across one side of the base of the glass.

2 Make two intertwining, curving lines in copper liner on the other side of the base, allowing them to bleed off the edges. Repeat around the bottom of the body of the glass.

3 Repeat this process on the base of the glass with single thick black lines followed by gold.

4 Once the black dots are dry, dab gold paint over them, using the end of the paintbrush.

5 Turn your glass upside down, and use the thick brush to paint the bottom of the base with silver paint.

6 Follow the paint manufacturer's instructions for either drying or baking the paint.

MATERIALS *and* TOOLS

- **10-inch (25.4 cm) glass plate**
- **Wineglass**
- **Mild detergent**
- **Surface conditioner (if recommended by the paint manufacturer)**
- **Sheet of white paper**
- **Scissors**
- **Glass liner paints: black, gold, copper**
- **Opaque glass paint: silver, black**
- **Artist's palette or old ceramic plate**
- **Pencil**
- **Large thick brush**

DESIGNER: **Nicky Painter**

Sunset Swirl Glasses

Use a simple technique to swirl together bright paints that create beautiful effects on these glasses.

INSTRUCTIONS

1 Wash and dry the glasses. Apply surface conditioner if recommended for use with your paint.

2 Squeeze out a portion of each of the paints onto the artist's palette or ceramic plate.

3 Turn one of the glasses upside down on the work surface.

4 Dab generous portions of each color onto the body of the glass in several places around the circumference. Use the other hand to grasp the stem of the glass.

5 Place a paintbrush at just above the stem on the bulb of the glass, and slowly spin the glass as you work the brush downward toward the rim. After you finish swirling the color on the main portion of the glass, allow it to dry thoroughly.

6 Flip the glass over and paint the stem of it in a swirl of colors, or in a mixture of a couple of the colors.

7 Repeat steps 3 through 6 to paint the other glass.

8 Follow the paint manufacturer's instructions for either drying or baking the paint.

Note: Since the rims of the glasses are covered with paint, they are not food safe, and should be used for decorative purposes only.

MATERIALS and TOOLS

- **2 wineglasses**
- **Mild detergent**
- **Surface conditioner (if recommended by the paint manufacturer)**
- **Glass paints: dark orange, fluorescent orange, brick red, yellow, copper**
- **Artist's palette or old ceramic plate**
- **Several thick, soft brushes**

DESIGNER: Nicky Painter

Stamped Leaf Vase

Dried leaf skeletons are used to stamp a layered, organic-looking surface on the voluptuous curves of this vase.

MATERIALS *and* TOOLS

- **Large glass vase**
- **Mild detergent**
- **Surface conditioner (if recommended by the paint manufacturer)**
- **Frosted glass paint in color of your choice for overall color of vase (we used green)**
- **Large flat brush**
- **Old newspapers**
- **Dried leaf skeletons (available at some art and craft stores)**
- **Artist's palette or old ceramic plate**
- **Opaque glass paints in a variety of colors of your choice (we used several shades of red, orange, yellow, and green)**
- **Wedge cosmetic sponges**

INSTRUCTIONS

1. Wash and dry the vase. Apply surface conditioner if recommended for use with your paint.

2. Paint over the entire surface of the vase (including the lip and the bottom) with a coat of the frosted glass paint. Allow the paint to dry, and add a second coat if you wish to darken the color. (This color will serve as the background for your leaf prints.)

3. Squeeze out small portions of the opaque paints onto your palette or plate.

4. Spread newspapers on your work surface. Lay out a few of the leaf skeletons.

5. Load one of the cosmetic sponges with paint, and dab it onto the leaf, covering the whole surface. Use a clean sponge to sponge away any excess paint that might glob and smear the print of the leaf.

6. Lift the leaf off the newspaper by one corner, and gently place it on the surface of the vase. Spread the leaf flat against the surface with your fingers or a clean sponge, then gently lift it off to reveal a stamp of the leaf. (If you find that you have trouble producing a good print, try practicing with the leaf on a piece of paper to figure out how much paint coverage you need.)

7. Continue to print with the leaves, using various colors and overlapping many prints. Build up layers of paint until you like the complexity of the surface. Print as much or as little of the vase as you like.

8. Once you're satisfied with the look of the vase, follow the paint manufacturer's instructions for either drying or baking the paint.

DESIGNER: Katherine Aimone

Etched Wave Lamps

A simple, elegant design painted in etched-effect paint creates the look of real etched glass.

MATERIALS *and* TOOLS

- **3 triangular or square glass oil lamps**
- **Mild detergent**
- **Surface conditioner (if recommended by the paint manufacturer)**
- **Wave template, enlarged to fit width of your lamp (see page 91)**
- **Scissors**
- **Self-adhesive vinyl with peel-off backing**
- **Pencil**
- **White etched-effect or frosted glass paint in a bottle**
- **Medium round brush with a good point**
- **Craft knife**

INSTRUCTIONS

1 Wash and dry the oil lamps. Apply surface conditioner if recommended for use with your paint.

2 Cut out the wave template, and trace it three times on the front of the vinyl. Cut out the patterns.

3 Line up the oil lamps.

4 Peel away the backing from the vinyl templates, and position the templates on the three bottles in ascending heights. (Keep in mind that you'll be painting below the adhered template.)

6 Paint the etching or frosted paint on each bottle beneath the wave template and down to the bottom of the bottle. Allow it to dry, and apply a second coat if needed.

7 Use the craft knife to cut a line in the paint along the edge of the vinyl on each wave. (Doing this will remove any paint bridges that may have formed.) Gently pull the vinyl off the bottle to reveal your design.

8 Paint the remaining sides of the bottles with a coat or two of the white paint.

9 Follow the paint manufacturer's instructions for either drying or baking the paint.

DESIGNER: Diana Light

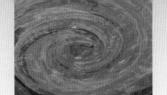

Wedding Bowl

The unusual design for this bowl was conceived by the designer as a wedding gift bearing the name of the happy couple. The gold lines on the bowl spell out "Aimone." Apply this idea to any name, and personalize such a piece for a wedding or anniversary gift.

MATERIALS *and* TOOLS

- Large decorative bowl with small base and wide rim
- Mild detergent
- Surface conditioner (if recommended by the paint manufacturer)
- White paper
- Pencil
- Artist's palette or old ceramic plate
- Transparent glass paints in colors of your choice
- Scissors
- Medium flat brush
- Water-based marking pen in dark color
- Small round brush with good tip
- Paper towels

INSTRUCTIONS

1 Wash and dry the bowl. Apply surface conditioner to the outside of the bowl if recommended for use with your paint.

2 On a sheet or sheets of white paper, use a pencil to write out the name that you'd like to paint on the bowl in longhand. Make the lines large and loopy. The name should be written large enough to span the outside of the bowl and fill the center portion of it. (If it's a short name, you can repeat the name, or add a first name to it.)

3 Apply paints to your palette or plate, and pick up one of the darker paints with the medium flat brush. Paint over the name you wrote on paper to create wide lines. Allow the paint to dry.

4 Cut the name out into several smaller segments. Tape the peices of the name together facedown to the inside of your bowl so that you can see lines through the walls of the bowl.

5 Turn the bowl over on its rim. Outline the letters (following your template) with the dark water-based pen.

6 Load the small round brush with a paint color of your choice, and fill in the letters of the name with one or more of the paints. Allow the paint to dry.

7 Using the letters that you've painted as the springboard for your design, draw relating abstract designs around the letters in the form of swirls, spirals, waves, and other doodles. If you draw something and don't like it, wipe it away with a paper towel and start again.

8 Once you create an overall design that you like, use both brushes to paint each section with solid areas of paint until the outer surface of the bowl is decorated with interlocking curved designs.

9 Follow the paint manufacturer's instructions for either drying or baking the paint.

DESIGNER: **Brenda Star**

Sun Lantern

Hot textured colors glow like balls of fire when lighted inside this glass-paned lantern.

INSTRUCTIONS

1 Clean the cut pieces of glass with glass cleaner. Apply surface conditioner to one side of each piece if recommended for use with your paint.

2 Cut off 16 strips of metallic tape. Apply a strip to each of the 16 sides of the glass, and smooth the strips into place, overlapping them at the corners. Pay attention to creating straight lines with the tape on the front of each piece.

3 Place a glass piece on top of each of the sun patterns, and trace each with white glass liner. Allow the paint to dry thoroughly.

4 Drip red and yellow transparent paint into the rays of the sun on each piece. Blend the paints together with a craft stick.

5 Squeeze portions of the amber, yellow, and red textured glass paint into the centers of the suns. Swirl and blend the paints with the craft stick, leaving a textured surface.

6 Squeeze clear and cobalt blue textured glass paints into the background of the pieces, and blend them together with a craft stick.

7 Allow the pieces to dry thoroughly on a flat surface. Follow the paint manufacturer's instructions for either drying or baking the paint.

8 Stand up two of the sides and position them at a 90-degree angle as you wish them to appear in the assembled piece. Place one of the cut dowels along the outside seam where the two pieces of glass meet, and tape it into place with a piece of metallic foil tape the same length as the seam. (The tape will conceal the dowel.)

9 Repeat the previous step to add dowels and tape the other three seams of the lantern.

10 Lift the lantern and position it around the wooden board. Place the candle in the center.

DESIGNER: **Alice Disney Huelskamp**

MATERIALS and TOOLS

- Glass cut into 10-inch-square (25.4 cm) pieces
- Spray glass cleaner
- Surface conditioner (if recommended for use with your paint)
- Metallic foil tape (available at glass supply and craft stores)
- Scissors
- Sun templates (see page 91)
- White glass liner
- Transparent glass paint: red, yellow
- Craft sticks
- Textured glass paint (gel): amber, yellow, red, clear, cobalt blue
- Palette knife
- 4 pieces of 1/8-inch (3 mm) dowel cut to the height of the glass pieces
- Flat wood board cut to fit flush inside the lantern
- Large square candle

Frosty Mugs

Even before you take a sip, you'll get a cool thrill from these frosty mugs.

41

MATERIALS *and* TOOLS

- **3 glass mugs of different shapes and sizes**
- **Mild detergent**
- **Surface conditioner (if recommended by the paint manufacturer)**
- **Round notebook paper reinforcers**
- **Opaque white glass paint**
- **White frosted or etched-effect glass paint**
- **Artist's palette or old ceramic plate**
- **Liner brush**
- **Wedge cosmetic sponges**
- **Paper towels**
- **Craft knife**
- **Frosted glass paints: bright green, cobalt blue**
- **Cotton swabs**
- **Masking tape**

INSTRUCTIONS
for GREEN-HANDLED MUG

1. Wash and dry the mugs. Apply surface conditioner if recommended for use with your paints.

2. Randomly stick notebook paper reinforcements to the lower half of the mug.

3. Pour out a bit of opaque white paint and a puddle of white frost paint onto your palette or plate. Use the liner brush to paint a wavy line around the mug above the page reinforcements. Allow the line to dry slightly.

4. Pick up some white frost paint with a sponge, and pat off the excess paint on a paper towel. Use a quick, repetitive motion to apply the paint lightly on the lower half of the mug beneath the drawn line. Allow the paint to dry for about an hour, and then apply a second coat.

5. Carefully remove the paper reinforcements. If the paint begins to pull up, cut around each reinforcement with the craft knife to break any paint bridges that may have formed.

6. Pour out a puddle of bright green frost paint onto your palette, and apply it with a sponge to the handle and foot of the mug. Allow the paint to dry thoroughly, and then apply a second coat.

7. Use the liner brush to paint a white opaque line between the foot and the main section of the mug and around the two joints where the handle attaches to the mug. Use a cotton swab to dab white opaque dots in the center of the circular reinforcements and on any portion of the handle that you'd like to decorate with dots.

DESIGNER: Alice Disney Huelskamp

INSTRUCTIONS
for BLUE FROSTED MUG

1 Apply a piece of masking tape around the top of the mug, at least ½ inch (1.3 cm) from the rim. Smooth the lower edge of the tape with your fingernail.

2 Pour some cobalt blue frost paint onto your palette. Sponge the bottom half of the mug with blue paint that follows a dipping, wavy line. Allow the paint to dry thoroughly, and apply a second coat.

3 Pour a puddle of white frost paint onto the palette. Dip the blunt end of one of the sponges in the paint, and use the sponge to paint wide lines all the way around the mug beneath the masking tape down to the blue paint. Place the lines at different angles with about ¼ to ½ inch (6 mm to 1.3 cm) between them. Allow the paint to dry thoroughly, and apply a second coat of white frost.

4 Use a liner brush and opaque white paint to outline the wide frosted lines, allowing the brushstrokes to overlap the blue frosted area.

INSTRUCTIONS
for BLUE AND GREEN FROSTED MUG

1 Use a sponge to apply frosted cobalt blue paint to the handle and the foot of the mug. Allow the paint to dry thoroughly, and apply a second coat. Use a sponge to apply a band of bright green paint to the section of the mug that joins the main section of the mug and the foot.

2 Paint stripes or other designs of your choice on the body of the mug with white frost paint. Allow the first coat to dry thoroughly, and then apply a second coat. Use the liner brush and opaque white to outline the stripes and add accent strokes to the design.

3 Use the liner brush to paint a white opaque stripe down the middle of the handle.

4 Follow the paint manufacturer's instructions for either drying or baking the paint on the three mugs.

Simple But Beautiful Vase

Random lines filled with color turn a plain glass vase into a work of art.

MATERIALS and TOOLS

- **Round glass vase**
- **Mild detergent**
- **Surface conditioner (if recommended for use by the paint manufacturer)**
- **Gold glass paint liner**
- **Cotton swabs**
- **Transparent glass paints: green, dark blue, and light blue**

INSTRUCTIONS

1. Wash and dry the vase. Apply surface conditioner if recommended for use with your paints.

2. Hold the vase by its base and tilt it. Choose an area near the top of the vase where you want to place an overlapping design, and begin squeezing the gold liner in a horizontal wavy line while you turn the vase. If you make a line you don't like, wipe it off with a moistened cotton swab, and continue the line where you left off. Don't worry about making lines that look perfect.

3. Once you've circled the vase, circle around again with another line or two, making a continuous, unbroken line. Allow the lines to overlap randomly.

4. If you wish, add another decorative band of overlapping lines to the bottom of the vase without breaking the lines (so that segmented areas will dam the colored paint later). Allow the paint bands to dry completely.

5. Turn the vase on its side. Drip various colors of glass paint into the small, segmented areas created by the lines, and keep the vase turned on its side while the colors dry. Allow an area to dry, then turn the vase to work on another side. Leave some of the areas blank as a contrast to the colored areas.

DESIGNER: Alice Disney Huelskamp

43

Faux Metallic Frame

A woven pattern of gold, silver, copper, and lead paints provides a textured backdrop for a favorite photo.

45

MATERIALS *and* TOOLS

- **Grid design template (see page 92)**
- **Double glass frame or document frame that holds paper between pieces of clear glass**
- **Photo**
- **Scissors**
- **Spray glass cleaner**
- **Glass liner: gold, silver, copper, lead**
- **Sheet of white paper**

INSTRUCTIONS

1 Enlarge the template to a size that fits your frame (you can trim the edges if needed because the template is an overall pattern.)

2 Cut the template to the size of the frame.

3 Remove the two pieces of glass, and clean them with glass cleaner.

4 Place the template faceup between the two pieces of glass, and place them back in the frame so that the lines show through the front piece of glass.

5 Practice using the black outliner on a sheet of paper to get a feel for it. (To begin making a line, squeeze the paint out of the tip, and touch the tip to the glass. When you reach the end of the line, lift the tip off the glass about ¼ inch [6 mm] while still squeezing, allowing the line to fall to the surface).

6 Begin drawing lines of paint on the glass by laying a black rectangular shape that is the size of your photo. Follow the lines of the grid to place the line.

7 Next, draw in a series of black vertical lines in the frame's border by following the grid. Allow the paint to dry before proceeding.

8 On top of the black lines, layer gold lines in a diagonal pattern by following the grid.

9 After you've allowed the gold lines to dry, lay the copper lines on top in a horizontal pattern by following the grid.

10 After the copper lines have dried, lay a series of silver lines on top of all the lines to create a woven look.

11 Follow the paint manufacturer's instructions for either drying or baking the paint.

DESIGNER: Diana Light

Miami Spice Bottles

Add spices or bath powders to these colorful bottes, or simply set them on a windowsill for a visual treat.

INSTRUCTIONS *for* STAR BOTTLE

1. Wash and dry the spice bottles, and apply surface conditioner if recommended for use with your paint.

2. Cut stars out of self-adhesive vinyl and apply them to one of the bottles as you wish. Smooth the stars into place.

3. Pour out bright green and cobalt blue paints onto the palette or plate. Dip the cosmetic sponge into the paint, and pat the excess paint off on a paper towel.

4. Sponge the bottle with the paint by using a quick, repetitive motion. Allow the paint to dry, and apply as many coats as you like until the desired color is achieved.

5. Carefully cut around the stars with the craft knife before removing them to create a clean edge.

6. Use the liner brush and cobalt blue paint to outline the stars.

INSTRUCTIONS *for* TRIANGLE BOTTLE

1. Cut a cosmetic sponge into a triangular shape that fits the size of the bottle.

2. Dip the sponge in bright green paint, pat off the excess on a paper towel, and stamp triangles as desired on the bottle. Allow the first coat to dry, and then restamp the triangles until you've achieved a color that you like.

3. Outline the triangles with a liner brush and cobalt blue paint.

MATERIALS *and* TOOLS

- **4 square-sided glass spice bottles**
- **Mild detergent**
- **Surface conditioner (if recommended by the paint manufacturer)**
- **Self-adhesive vinyl with peel-off backing**
- **Scissors**
- **Frosted glass paints: bright green, cobalt blue**
- **Artist's palette or old ceramic plate**
- **Wedge cosmetic sponges**
- **Paper towels**
- **Craft knife**
- **Liner brush**
- **¼-inch-wide (6 mm) masking tape**
- **Cotton swabs**
- **Hole punch**
- **Thin silver wire**
- **Wire cutters**
- **Beads**
- **Chopstick**

DESIGNER: Alice Disney Huelskamp

INSTRUCTIONS
for STRIPED BOTTLE

1. Apply vertical strips of masking tape side by side to all sides of the bottle. Remove every other piece of tape to reveal a stripe pattern. Smooth the tape into place.

2. Dip the sponge into cobalt blue and sponge-paint the stripes. Allow the paint to dry, and then apply additional coats as desired. Carefully remove the tape, using the craft knife to cut through any paint bridges that may have formed.

3. Use a cotton swab to sponge random dots between the lines with green paint.

INSTRUCTIONS
for POLKA-DOT BOTTLE

1. Cut out a piece of self-adhesive paper the same height as the bottle and wide enough to wrap around the bottle four times. Make random holes with the hole punch, reserving the pieces that fall out.

2. Position the self-adhesive paper on the sides of the bottle and smooth it out.

3. Using a sponge and cobalt blue paints, stencil the dots. Allow the paint to dry, and reapply until the desired color is achieved. Carefully remove self-adhesive paper to reveal the dot pattern.

4. Use the liner brush and green paint to make random vertical lines on each side between and connecting the dots.

INSTRUCTIONS
for GREEN POLKA-DOT BOTTLE

1. Position self-adhesive paper fallouts on the bottles, and smooth the dots with your fingertips.

2. Pour out a puddle of light green and cobalt blue paints onto the palette or plate. Dip the sponge into both colors and gently blend the mixture on the palette. Sponge the color onto the bottle over the dots.

3. After the paint has dried, apply additional coats as needed to achieve the desired color. Remove the self-adhesive dots.

4. Use a cotton swab and cobalt blue to make random dots on top of the painted surface.

5. Follow the paint manufacturer's instructions for either drying or baking the paint on the bottles.

ADDING WIRE AND BEADS

1. Cut off strips of silver wire that fit around the necks of the bottles several times, with extra length for adding beads and curling the wires.

2. Wrap wire around the neck of a bottle, and twist the ends of the wire together close to the surface of the bottle to hold them in place.

3. Slide beads onto the ends of the wire, and then curl each of the ends around the tip of the chopstick to create curls to hold the beads in place.

4. Manipulate the wire as you wish.

Silver and Gold Elegance

Make an occasion out of afternoon tea or coffee with these tastefully adorned cups and plates.

MATERIALS and TOOLS

- **Mild detergent**
- **Surface conditioner (if recommended for use by the paint manufacturer)**
- **Glass plate, saucer, and plate**
- **Artist's palette or old ceramic plate**
- **Glass paints: gold, silver**
- **Small and medium paintbrushes**

INSTRUCTIONS

1 Wash and dry the glassware. Apply surface conditioner to the backs of the plate and saucer and the sides of the cup if recommended for use with your paints.

2 Squeeze out a bit of gold and a bit of silver paint onto your palette or plate.

3 Turn the plate over, and paint a rim design of small gold squares, leaving spaces between them (see finished photo). Paint a gold line that defines the border of the band of squares.

4 Allow the paint to dry. Within the gold boundary line, paint a background behind the squares with silver paint. (You can cover the squares with the paint, and it won't show on the front.)

5 Use the same idea to paint a design of squares on the bottom of the cup.

6 On the back of the saucer, paint fanning stripes with gold and silver paints.

7 Follow the paint manufacturer's instructions for either drying or baking the paint.

DESIGNER: Tana Boerger

49

Bamboo Vase

Rough bamboo shapes outlined with white paint against a frosted background create a beautiful complement for this curved vase.

MATERIALS
and TOOLS

- Glass vase with convex shape
- Mild detergent
- Surface conditioner (if recommended by the paint manufacturer)
- Bamboo template (see page 92)
- Masking tape
- Opaque glass paints: amber, kelly green, white
- Artist's palette or old ceramic plate
- Medium flat brush
- Small round brush
- White frosted glass paint
- Wedge cosmetic sponges
- Liner brush

INSTRUCTIONS

1. Wash and dry the vase. Apply surface conditioner if recommended for use with your paints.

2. Position variations of the template (repeating them as you wish) inside the vase and secure them with masking tape.

3. Squeeze out small portions of the opaque paints on the palette or plate.

4. Use the medium flat brush to roughly fill in the bamboo stalks with several coats of amber paint, allowing the paint to dry between coats.

5. Use the small round brush to mix together a bit of amber paint and kelly green paint. Roughly paint in the shapes of the leaves by pulling the brush from the tip of the leaf backward and then up. Apply additional coats as needed, allowing the paint to dry between coats.

6. Apply white frosted paint to the palette or plate, and load a sponge with it. Apply paint to the background (around the stalks and leaves) with a quick, repetitive motion. Allow the paint to dry completely, and then apply another coat.

7. Load the liner brush with opaque white paint. Referring to the finished photo of the vase, paint in the outlines of the bamboo shoots and leaves.

8. Follow the paint manufacturer's instructions for either drying or baking the paint.

DESIGNER: Alice Disney Huelskamp

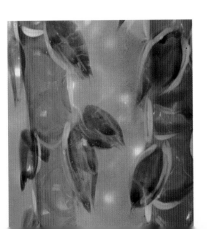

Lascaux-Inspired Plates

Ancient motifs look contemporary on these cave-painting-inspired plates.

MATERIALS and TOOLS

- **3 glass plates of graduated sizes (we used a 14-inch [35.6 cm] plate, a 10-inch [25.4 cm] plate, and an 8-inch [20.3 cm] plate)**
- **Mild detergent**
- **Surface conditioner (if recommended by the paint manufacturer)**
- **Animal-image rubber stamps of your choice in graduated sizes to fit within the rims of your plates**
- **Several sheets of white paper**
- **Pencil**
- **Stamp pad in dark color for mock-up of designs**
- **Masking tape**
- **Small pointed round brush for painting details and outlines**
- **Bottle of permanent black ink**
- **Medium round brush**
- **Glass paints: reddish brown, mustard yellow or other earth-tone colors of your choice**

INSTRUCTIONS

1. Wash and dry the plates. Apply surface conditioner if recommended for use with your paint.

2. Decide which of the stamps you want to use on each plate (we used larger stamps on the largest plate, for instance). Mix and match the stamps if you want, keeping in mind how the plates will look when they're nested.

3. Trace each of the plates onto a sheet of white paper. With your pencil, sketch a circle within each plate's outline to indicate the width of each of the rims. Within these bands, stamp repeating images with your rubber stamps and stamp pad. When you're happy with the placement of the designs, cut each animal or group of animals out with your scissors and position the images face-down on the fronts of the plates. Tape them into place with masking tape.

4. Use the small brush and the permanent ink (straight from the bottle) to loosely outline the images that you see through the glass. Don't worry about making the lines look perfect; make them look sketchy. Paint in any details within the images. Add any accent marks between the images (such as dots) with the black ink. Allow the ink to dry.

5. Use the medium brush to paint colors with glass paints within the lines that you've drawn.

6. Follow the paint manufacturer's instructions for either drying or baking the paint.

DESIGNER: Luann Udell

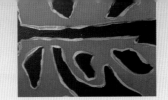

Chinese Love Vase

Inscribe a vase with the beautiful form of a Chinese character.

INSTRUCTIONS

1. Wash and dry the vase. Apply surface conditioner if recommended for use with your paints.

2. Cut out the paper template, and trace the character onto the paper side of the self-adhesive vinyl. Use the craft knife to cut out sections to form a stencil.

3. Carefully remove the paper backing from the stencil, and position it on the vase. Overlap and smooth the vinyl, cutting small slits in the template as needed to fit the curve of the vase.

4. Squeeze out a portion of black paint onto the palette. Dip a cosmetic sponge into the paint, pat off the excess on the palette, and paint the character with a quick, repetitive motion. Allow the paint to dry. Apply several light coats of paint this way.

5. Carefully remove the stencil. If the paint begins to lift, carefully cut around the stencil openings with the craft knife. Allow the paint to dry thoroughly.

6. On the palette, use the palette knife to mix three parts frosted bright green with one part frosted bright red to make a dark green paint. Use a clean cosmetic sponge to paint the entire vase, going over the stencil. Allow paint to dry thoroughly, and apply a second coat with the sponge.

7. After the paint has dried, paint on another heavy coat with the 1-inch (2.5 cm) flat brush, leaving uneven color with the brushstrokes. Allow the paint to dry thoroughly.

8. Outline the character with the liner brush and gold paint. Use a sponge to color the rim with gold.

9. Follow the paint manufacturer's instructions for either drying or baking the paint.

DESIGNER: Alice Disney Huelsckamp

MATERIALS and TOOLS

- **Large glass vase**
- **Mild detergent**
- **Surface conditioner (if recommended by the paint manufacturer)**
- **Chinese character template (see page 92)**
- **Pencil**
- **Self-adhesive vinyl with paper backing**
- **Craft knife**
- **Opaque glass paints: black, gold**
- **Wedge cosmetic sponges**
- **Palette knife**
- **Artist's palette or old ceramic plate**
- **Frosted glass paints: bright green, bright red**
- **1-inch (2.5 cm) flat brush**
- **Liner brush**

Stamped and Painted Pins

Stamped images and simple brushstrokes turn pieces of cut glass into elegant evening pins.

INSTRUCTIONS

1 Apply surface conditioner to the glass shapes if recommended for use with your paint.

2 Ink and stamp one side of each glass piece with permanent ink (black or gold). Don't slide or rock the stamp, or your image will be blurred. If you use a solid image, and it doesn't stamp completely, use a paintbrush and ink to fill in the incomplete parts of the image. (If you do this, be sure to clean the stamp and brush immediately, because the permanent ink dries very quickly.) Allow the stamped image to dry completely.

3 Use a medium round paintbrush and glass paint to swipe splashes of color onto the glass on the same side that you stamped.

4 Follow the paint manufacturer's instructions for either drying or baking the paint.

5 Thin the white glue slightly with water so that it can be brushed easily onto the glass. Brush an even coat of glue over the stamped side of each piece of glass, and then place the cardstock on top of the pins. Smooth the paper and press out any bubbles. Allow the glue to dry thoroughly.

6 Use the craft knife to trim away the excess paper from the edges of the pins.

7 Apply metallic foil tape to the edges by centering a strip of it on one side of one pin and carefully smoothing the tape around the entire edge. Overlap the edges slightly. Press the tape toward the front and back of each pin with the edge of a pencil or a fingernail, smoothing around the curves if necessary. The tape creates a frame for the pin and finishes the edges.

8 Glue a pin back in the center of each pin with strong craft glue or epoxy.

Stamp Credits: Dragonfly background (Magenta), dragon (Stamp Francisco), Asian seals (Hero Arts), bamboo (Stamp Francisco)

DESIGNER: Lynn B. Krucke

MATERIALS and TOOLS

- **Thin glass sheet, cut into geometric shapes of your choice for use as pins. (A stained glass supply shop or a mirror and glass supplier should be able to cut the glass into the shapes you want for a minimal fee, and grind the edges for you.)**

- **Surface conditioner (if recommended by the paint manufacturer)**

- **Permanent ink pads in black and gold**

- **Assorted rubber stamps (you will be creating a reverse image, so avoid stamps with writing on them)**

- **Medium round paintbrush**

- **Glass paints in colors of your choice**

- **White craft glue that dries clear**

- **Glue brush**

- **Sheet of cardstock**

- **Craft knife**

- **Metallic foil tape (available at stained glass supply and craft stores)**

- **3 pin backs**

- **Strong craft glue or epoxy**

Bright Frosted Glasses and Ice Bucket

Icy blues and greens contrast with hot pinks and yellows to compose jazzy geometrics on these fun pieces.

INSTRUCTIONS

1. Wash and dry the glassware. Apply surface conditioner if recommended for your use with your paints.

2. Apply pieces of masking tape around the top edges of the glasses and the ice bucket. Refer to the photo to divide the surfaces of the glasses and the ice bucket into randomly shaped sections with masking tape. Smooth the edges of the tapes with your fingernail.

3. Pour out puddles of frosted paints onto the palette or plate. Dip a cosmetic sponge into one of the colors. Sponge several sections with a quick, repetitive motion. Use the small paintbrush to paint the bases in a color of your choice.

4. Allow the paint to dry, then apply a second coat with the sponge and the brush.

5. Use the same procedure to paint the remaining sections and the stems with two coats of paint. Allow the paint to dry.

6. Use the craft knife to cut a line in the paint along the edge of the masking tape in each section. (Doing this will remove any paint bridges that may have formed over the tape.) Carefully pull the tape away from the glass. Use the craft knife to scrape off any excess paint.

7. Use the liner brush and white pearl paint to outline each colored section. Paint frosted spirals, dots, or stripes in various colors in each of the sections. Allow the paint to dry.

8. Follow the paint manufacturer's instructions for either drying or baking the paint.

DESIGNER: **Alice Disney Huelskamp**

MATERIALS *and* TOOLS

- **Wineglasses with interesting stems**
- **Glass ice bucket**
- **Mild detergent**
- **Surface conditioner (if recommended by the paint manufacturer)**
- **½-inch (1.3 cm) masking tape**
- **Frosted glass paints: cobalt blue, bright red or hot pink, bright yellow, bright green**
- **Artist's palette or old ceramic plate**
- **Wedge cosmetic sponges**
- **Small rounded brush**
- **Craft knife**
- **Liner brush**
- **White pearl glass paint**

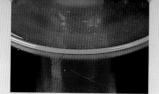

Festive Candlesticks

Blend two transparent paint colors together on the surfaces of these candleholders to create a shimmering effect.

INSTRUCTIONS

1 Wash and dry the candleholders. Apply surface conditioner if recommended for use with your paints.

2 Hold one of the candleholders by its top, and turn it upside down.

3 Load the brush with yellow paint, and pull broad strokes down from the bottom of the candlestick base to the break where the sphere sits. Leave the brushstrokes as they happen.

4 While the yellow paint is still wet, load the brush with red and repeat step 3, leaving some yellow areas and creating some blended yellow-red (orange) areas.

5 Allow the paint to dry.

6 Paint the sphere red.

7 With the candlestick upside down on your work surface, paint the bottom of it with yellow. Allow all paint to dry.

8 Repeat the previous steps to paint the second candleholder.

9 Follow the paint manufacturer's instructions for either drying or baking the paint.

DESIGNER: Diana Light

MATERIALS *and* TOOLS

- **Two short, fluted glass candleholders with spherical shapes in center**
- **Mild detergent**
- **Surface conditioner (if recommended by the paint manufacturer)**
- **¼-inch (6 mm) flat brush**
- **Transparent glass paints: yellow, red**

Sgraffito Peacock Plate

This elegant plate is made with the simplest techniques.

MATERIALS and TOOLS

- Glass plate in size of your choice
- Mild detergent
- Surface conditioner (if recommended by the paint manufacturer)
- Artist's palette or old ceramic plate
- Glass paints: black, navy blue, turquoise, pea green
- 2 thick, soft brushes
- Wedge cosmetic sponges

INSTRUCTIONS

1 Wash and dry the plate. Apply surface conditioner if recommended for use with your paint.

2 Squeeze out small portions of the glass paints onto the palette or ceramic plate.

3 Begin in the center of the plate on the back, and use one of the paintbrushes to swipe a circular center of black paint. As you work outward toward the edge of the plate, gradually work in navy blue paint, followed by turquoise paint. Finish the edge with pea green paint.

4 Position the clean brush in the center of the plate. Swipe and blend the paint again. (Do this quickly before the paint starts to dry.)

5 With the other end of the brush, draw a line through the middle that begins at one edge and goes all the way across.

6 Use this line as your starting point to make more slightly curved lines fanning out toward the top of your plate. As you work your way down the center line, space the lines farther apart to create a featherlike effect. Repeat this process on both sides of your center line.

7 Allow the paint to dry for about an hour before sponging a layer of pea green paint over the design.

8 Follow the paint manufacturer's instructions for either drying or baking the paint.

DESIGNER: **Nicky Painter**

Stripes with Stars Bottles

Bannerlike stripes that are sprayed on to create a smooth painted surface wind playfully up the sides of these giant bottles.

INSTRUCTIONS

1 Wind the tape measure in a loose spiral around one of the bottles from top to bottom to estimate how long of a stripe it will take to decorate the bottle from the base to the top. Cut two 1-inch-wide (2.5 cm) strips of vinyl of this length.

2 On one side of each of the strips, draw a loose, slightly wavy line with the pencil. Cut along this line with the scissors and remove the excess vinyl.

3 Place the two strips right-side-up on your work surface with the curved portions facing each other. Peel a portion of the backing off the bottom of each of the strips.

4 Beginning at the base of the bottle, place the curved insides of each of the ends of the strips together. Adhere the strips to the bottle, and then gradually widen them into a channel as you begin to move up the bottle.

5 As you curve the strips around the bottle in a spiral, you'll have to make the line change directions in order to make them fit. Cut small slits in the width of the vinyl on the noncurved sides that allow you to bend the line.

6 Cut out the star templates, and trace several of each size onto the vinyl. Cut them out with the craft knife. Save the leftover pieces of vinyl for later. Apply the stars in a random pattern between the vinyl strips.

7 Randomly cut pieces of vinyl to cover the rest of the bottle in the areas outside the stripe (on either side of the curved strips). Stick on the pieces in a patchwork fashion.

8 Once all the vinyl is in place and only the areas are exposed that you want to color, spray transparent glass paint on the exposed areas of each of the bottles and stoppers. (Make sure that you do this in a well-ventilated area, or, preferably, outside. The fumes can be hazardous.) If you wish, layer two or more colors of spray to create a graduated, rainbow-like effect on the stripes. For the best effect, use multiple light coats of paint that you allow to dry in between coats rather than one heavy coat.

9 Allow the paint to dry thoroughly before removing the vinyl masks.

DESIGNER: **Diana Light**

MATERIALS and TOOLS

- **2 oversized decorative colored bottles (available at some home decor or craft stores)**
- **Mild detergent**
- **Tape measure**
- **Scissors**
- **Self-adhesive vinyl with peel-off backing**
- **Pencil**
- **Star templates (see page 92)**
- **Craft knife**
- **Transparent spray paints for glass in colors of your choice**

Catalina Fishbowl

Reverse-paint fun watery creatures on the back of this bowl before encasing them in a sea of blue and green.

MATERIALS and TOOLS

- **Shallow glass bowl**
- **Mild detergent**
- **Surface conditioner (if recommended by the paint manufacturer)**
- **Sea life templates (page 94)**
- **Scissors**
- **Masking tape**
- **Black glass paint pen or glass paint liner**
- **Small, medium, and large artist's brushes**
- **Artist's palette or old ceramic plate**
- **Glass paints: yellow, orange, red, green, turquoise, blue, pink, maroon**

INSTRUCTIONS

1. Wash and dry the bowl. Apply surface conditioner if recommended for use with your paint.

2. Cut out the templates, and tape them facedown to the inside of the bowl. (You'll be painting the big, wide ocean, so place them wherever you like in their watery environment!)

3. Flip the bowl over, and use the thick, black paint to outline the shapes of your creatures. Draw some round circles with the paint in the surrounding waters to look like bubbles. Add other details with some black as you wish, keeping in mind that these will serve as your outlines when the piece is finished.

4. Dip the tip of one of your brush handles into black paint and make a dot for each fish's eye and a small rounded stroke of paint inside each bubble to give it dimension. On the large fish, draw a larger circle with the black paint around the dot to complete the eye. Add fins and other details on the fish with the black pen.

5. Squeeze out several bright colors onto your palette or plate. Use a small or medium brush to paint each fish with combinations of the colors. (To create depth, paint the lighter color on first, followed by the darker color.)

6. Repeat steps 1 through 5 to outline and paint the other creatures that you have taped to the inside of the bowl. Allow the paint to dry.

7. Dip your large brush into the green and turquoise paints and brush on large, wavy strokes to indicate water, blending the colors as you go. While the paint is still wet, paint and blend large strokes of blue paint to fill the ocean.

8. Follow the paint manufacturer's instructions for either drying or baking the paint.

DESIGNER: Nicky Painter

Retro Cookie Jar

Even if you weren't around to remember the fifties, this painted cookie jar is sure to make your day a happy one.

MATERIALS *and* TOOLS

- **Square glass cookie jar**
- **Mild detergent**
- **Surface conditioner (if recommended by the paint manufacturer)**
- **Opaque glass paints: turquoise, bright yellow, white, black, bright red**
- **Artist's palette or old ceramic plate**
- **2 flat compressed sponges**
- **Medium flat brush**
- **Liner brush**
- **Scissors**
- **Fruit templates (see page 92)**
- **Transfer paper**
- **Pencil**
- **Small round brush**

INSTRUCTIONS

1 Wash and dry the cookie jar. Apply surface conditioner if recommended for use with your paints.

2 Squeeze out small amounts of the glass paints onto your palette or plate.

3 Load one of the sponges with turquoise paint, and use it to sponge-paint the lid. Allow the paint to dry.

4 Load the medium flat brush with bright yellow paint, and paint a series of squares around the top of the lid close to the edge.

5 Use the liner brush to paint white lines on the side of the lid.

6 Use the medium flat brush to paint each of the square sides with a coat of white paint. Allow the paint to dry, and add a second coat if needed.

7 Use scissors to cut a 1-inch-square (2.5 cm) piece of flat sponge. Wet the sponge with water, and wring out the excess moisture. Dip the sponge in black paint, and stamp a pattern of black squares around the borders of the white squares (refer to finished photo for guidance). Allow the paint to dry thoroughly.

8 Use the template and transfer paper to lightly trace the cherry and apple designs onto the center of each square, alternating the designs.

9 Use the small round brush to paint the fruit with bright red paint, using the small round brush. Paint the stems black and the leaves turquoise. Paint in white highlights on the fruit and leaves.

10 Paint in accent colors on the sides of your jar and above the squares, as suggested by the shape of your jar.

11 Follow the paint manufacturer's instructions for either drying or baking the paint.

67

DESIGNER: Alice Disney Huelskamp

Silver Lining Cakestand

Fluffy clouds soft enough for an angel are revealed as you serve your favorite cake.

MATERIALS and TOOLS

Glass cakestand

Mild detergent

Surface conditioner (if recommended by the paint manufacturer)

Cloud templates (see page 93)

Scissors

Masking tape

Silver liner glass paint

Opaque glass paints: yellow, white, light blue

Artist's palette or old ceramic plate

Small round brush with good point

Wedge cosmetic sponges

Paper towels

Medium flat brush

INSTRUCTIONS

1 Wash and dry the cakestand. Apply surface conditioner if recommended for use with your paints.

2 Cut out the templates, and tape them facedown to the top surface of the cakestand. Allow some of them to run off the edges of the plate.

3 Turn the cakestand facedown on your work surface so that you can see the clouds through the glass. Outline them with the silver liner. Allow the liner to dry.

4 Squeeze portions of the glass paints onto your palette or plate. Use the small brush to paint small stars and triangles on the plate in yellow, using the finished piece as a guide. Allow the paint to dry.

5 On the artist's palette or ceramic plate, mix together a small amount of light blue paint with a larger amount of white paint to make a pale blue.

6 Dab the sponge in the light blue paint, and sponge the excess off on a paper towel. Sponge along the bottom of the clouds so that the blue overlaps the bottom of each cloud slightly.

7 Sponge white paint onto the rest of the cloud so that it slightly overlaps the pale blue and the lines on one side of each cloud. Allow the clouds to dry.

8 Use the medium flat brush to paint a coat of light blue paint over the backs of the clouds to serve as the background or sky.

9 Paint the stem and the underside of the base of the stem with yellow paint.

10 Follow the paint manufacturer's instructions for either drying or baking the paint.

69

DESIGNER: Diana Light

Hip Blender

Turn a plain glass blender into an anything-but-ordinary party machine.

INSTRUCTIONS

1. Wash and dry the glass blender top. Apply surface conditioner to the glass if recommended for use with your paint.

2. Cut circles out of the white paper of various sizes that range from ½ inch (1.3 cm) to 2 inches (5 cm).

3. Tape the circles inside the blender in a random pattern, juxtaposing different sizes. (Avoid placing circles in the areas where the glass is marked with measurements.)

4. Squeeze out some orange paint and a bit of white onto the palette or plate. On the outside of the blender, use the paper pieces as a guide to paint some of the larger circles with orange paint. Add a bit of white to the orange to lighten it, and paint the rest of the larger circles with light orange. Allow the paint to dry. After the paint dries about an hour, you can add a second coat if needed.

5. On a few of the orange circles, use a contrasting orange paint (lighter or darker) to add petal shapes to the circle (single brushstrokes that radiate from the center of the circle).

6. Squeeze out some avacado green paint and add a bit of white to it to lighten it to a lime green color. Paint the smallest circles with this color.

7. Connect some of the circles with green lines to make a treelike effect.

8. Follow the paint manufacturer's instructions for either drying or baking the paint.

DESIGNER: Diana Light

MATERIALS and TOOLS

- **Kitchen blender with glass top**
- **Mild detergent**
- **Surface conditioner (if recommended by paint manufacturer)**
- **White paper**
- **Scissors**
- **Masking tape**
- **Opaque glass paints: orange, white, avocado green**
- **Artist's palette or old ceramic plate**
- **Medium round brush**

Wildflower Platter

No matter how far away springtime is, you'll be cheered by the fresh painted flowers that adorn this platter.

INSTRUCTIONS

1 Wash and dry the platter. Apply surface conditioner if recommended for use with your paint.

2 Turn the platter over on your work surface so that you can paint on the back of it.

3 Use the fine artist's brush to paint red, rounded squiggle marks to be used as details in the round, orange flowers.

4 Repeat this process in orange along the edges of your red squiggle marks.

5 Once the red and orange marks are dry, use the medium brush to paint on a yellow background with rounded edges to make round, puffy flowers.

6 To paint the purple pom-pom flowers, use your smaller artist's brush. Begin in the center of each flower and make a quick stroke outward, repeating the strokes until each flower is full.

7 Dip your large brush in red followed by a touch of orange, and add rose-shaped flowers to the plate. While the paint is still wet, use the other end of your paintbrush to scratch petals and a blooming center in the paint.

8 To make the tall, pink and purple flowers, dip your small brush in purple paint and paint a series of fanning strokes from a common center. With pink paint and the medium brush, add less detailed strokes behind the pink ones to fill out the flower and create depth.

9 Dip your large brush in the yellow paint, followed by a touch of white in preparation for painting the large yellow flower near the center of the plate. Beginning at the center of the flower and working out, create several large petals to form a flower. While the paint is still wet, use the other end of the paintbrush to scratch a spiral shape in the center of the flower. Add other yellow flowers as you wish that bleed off the edge of the plate.

10 Use the medium paintbrush loaded with green paint to add stems that connect with the flowers and run off the edge of the plate. Add small green leaves along the stems and larger green leaves to the yellow flowers. Use the other end of your paintbrush to scratch veins onto some of the larger leaves.

11 Follow the paint manufacturer's instructions for either drying or baking the paint.

MATERIALS *and* TOOLS

- Glass oval platter
- Mild detergent
- Surface conditioner (if recommended by the paint manufacturer)
- Glass paints: red, orange, yellow, purple, green, pink, white
- Small, medium, and large round brushes

DESIGNER: **Nicky Painter**

Puzzle Bottles

These sculptured bottles that fit together like a puzzle provide a perfect opportunity for a geometric design complemented by sparkling glass baubles.

INSTRUCTIONS

1 Remove the corks from the bottles. Wash and dry the bottles. Apply surface conditioner if recommended for use with your paint.

2 Lay the bottles on their backs so that the front of each bottle faces you. Cut the paper into a diamond shape (or another shape of your choice) that fits the front of each bottle, and use the black pen to trace the shape onto each.

3 Outline the shape with the liner. Next, outline the front of each bottle close to the edge.

4 Use the liner to draw a straight line dividing the top of the face of each bottle from the bottom, skipping over the shape that you've drawn (if you have drawn a diamond, you'll extend this line from the points of the diamond). Make the lines the same height across the fronts of all the bottles.

5 Fill in the diamond or other shape on the front of each bottle with a continuous back-and-forth horizontal line made with the liner.

6 Grab a colored glass shape with the tweezers, and set it carefully into the wet outliner. Repeat this process to place a shape on each of the other bottles. Allow the liner to dry thoroughly. (The outliner will hold the shape in place after it dries.)

7 Apply the paints to your palette. Use the brush to paint on a different color in each outlined section on the front of each bottle, alternating the colors in the blocks so that the bottles have an overall design when placed side by side. Apply the paint rather thickly, and then even out the surface with smooth brushstrokes.

8 Follow the paint manufacturer's instructions for either drying or baking the paint.

DESIGNER: Diana Light

Tall Dogwood Vase and Small Flower Vases

Pretty pink dogwoods adorn the curved surface of a tall glass vase. Jelly glasses make sweet bud vases when adorned with a design of cheerful flowers and stripes.

INSTRUCTIONS
for DOGWOOD VASE

1 Wash and dry the vase. Apply surface conditioner if recommended for use with your paint.

2 Use masking tape to mask off several random squares on the surface of the vase. Smooth the edges of the tape.

3 Apply the paints to the artist's palette or ceramic plate. Load the sponge with some light blue paint, and use a quick, repetitive motion to sponge paint inside the square stencils. Allow the paint to dry, and apply a second coat if needed.

4 Load the round brush with fuchsia tipped with red paint. Blend the paint slightly on the palette. To paint flowers within the squares, set the brush down where the outside of the petal will be, then lift the brush as you pull toward the center of the petal. Add four more petals to make a pink dogwood flower. Repeat these steps to add dogwood flowers to the center of each of the squares and between the squares on the unpainted parts of the vase. Allow the paint to dry.

5 Use the liner brush to stipple several small white dots in the center of each of the flowers.

6 Clean the round brush, and load it with green paint. Add green petals to the flowers using the same motion that you did to create the petals.

7 Use the liner brush and white paint to paint wavy accent lines around the blue squares and a highlight line on each of the leaves.

8 Follow the paint manufacturer's instructions for either drying or baking the paint.

MATERIALS *and* TOOLS
for Dogwood Vase

- **Cylinder-shaped glass vase**
- **Mild detergent**
- **Surface conditioner (if recommended by the paint manufacturer)**
- **Masking tape**
- **Opaque glass paints: light blue, fuchsia, red, white, green**
- **Artist's palette or old ceramic plate**
- **Wedge cosmetic sponges**
- **Medium round brush**
- **Liner brush**

77

DESIGNER: **Alice Disney Huelskamp**

INSTRUCTIONS
for SMALL FLOWER VASE

1 Wash and dry the glassware. Apply surface conditioner if recommended for use with your paint.

2 Use strips of masking tape to mask off a background of stripes or geometric designs on the two vases. (Refer to the photos for suggestions.) Smooth down the edges of the tape.

3 Squeeze out small portions of the glass paints on the artist's palette or plate. Load one of the sponges with white or blue paint, and sponge paint into the masked areas with a quick, repetitive motion. Allow the paint to dry thoroughly. Carefully pull off the tape, using a craft knife to cut through any paint bridges that may have formed.

4 Dip the liner brush in green, and tip it with white paint before blending it lightly on the palette. Paint meandering green vines on top of the stripes on your vases.

5 To add leaves, dip the small round brush in green, and tip it with white before lightly blending it on the palette. Set the tip of the brush down at the base of each leaf, and lift the brush as you pull to form the tip of the leaf. Add as many leaves as you like to the vines. Allow the paint to dry.

6 Paint small flowers on top of the vines, using the smaller round brush for the small pink flowers and the medium round brush for the yellow flowers. Add white dots to the centers of the flowers.

7 To paint flowers that look like the larger pink flowers, load the flat brush with fuchsia tipped on one side with red and the other side with white. Blend the colors lightly on the palette. To paint each petal, place the red side of the brush in the center of the flower, and fan the brush around in the direction of the white side of the brush. Add small white dots in the center of each flower.

8 Follow the paint manufacturer's instructions for either drying or baking the paint.

MATERIALS *and* TOOLS
for Small Flower Vases

- **2 jelly glasses or small glass vases**
- **Mild detergent**
- **Surface conditioner (if recommended by the paint manufacturer)**
- **Masking tape**
- **Opaque glass paints: white, blue, green, fuchsia, red, bright yellow**
- **Artist's palette or old ceramic plate**
- **Wedge cosmetic sponges**
- **Craft knife**
- **Liner brush**
- **Small and medium round brushes**
- **Medium flat brush**

DESIGNER: Alice Disney Huelskamp

Leopard-Print Salt-and-Pepper Shakers

A leopard has kindly lent his spots to adorn this salt and pepper set that is oh-so-easy to paint.

MATERIALS and TOOLS

- **Set of square glass salt and pepper shakers**
- **Mild detergent**
- **Surface conditioner (if recommended by the paint manufacturer)**
- **Artist's palette or old ceramic plate**
- **Opaque glass paints: khaki/tan, brown, black**
- **Medium round brush**
- **Small brush with point**
- **Black paint pen or glass paint lines**

INSTRUCTIONS

1 Wash and dry the shakers. Apply surface conditioner if recommended for use with your paint.

2 Squeeze out small portions of the glass paints onto the artist's palette or ceramic plate.

3 Use the medium round brush to paint the body of one shaker with a coat of khaki/tan paint and the other shaker with a coat of brown. Allow the paints to dry thoroughly.

4 Use the medium round brush to paint the lids with a very light coat of black paint (avoid getting paint in the holes).

5 Use the small brush to randomly paint small lima bean shapes on the shakers in the following colors: khaki/tan on the brown shaker and brown on the khaki/tan shaker.

6 Once the paint is dry, outline the shapes with the black paint pen or liner.

7 Follow the paint manufacturer's instructions for either drying or baking the paint.

DESIGNER: Nicky Painter

Flower-Power Roll Cart

This splashy cart filled with cold drinks or cocktails is a handy as well as impressive way to serve your guests.

MATERIALS *and* TOOLS

- Round chrome rolling cart with glass shelves
- Spray glass cleaner
- Paper towels
- Surface conditioner (if recommended by paint manufacturer)
- Flower template (page 94)
- Masking tape
- Opaque silver liner for glass
- Air-dry transparent glass paints: red, dark purple, and green
- Artist's palette or old ceramic plate
- Matt medium
- Small round brush
- Large round brush
- Spray glass paints: blue and red

INSTRUCTIONS

1 Lift the top glass shelf carefully from the cart.

2 Clean it with the glass cleaner to remove smudges. Apply surface conditioner if recommended for use with your paints.

3 Place the design template underneath the glass, and anchor it with tape on the edges.

4 Outline the lines of the template with the silver outliner. Allow the lines to dry thoroughly.

5 Squeeze out a portion of transparent purple paint on the artist's palette or plate, and paint in the centers of the flowers with the paint. (Don't worry if the paint spills onto the the outliner because it won't show on the front when you turn the piece over.)

6 Apply transparent red to your palette and mix in a bit of matt medium. Use the large brush to paint in the petals on the flowers, moving the paint quickly enough that it doesn't dry before you've filled it in. Use the smaller brush to get paint into the corners of the petals.

7 Apply green transparent paint to your palette and mix in a bit of matt medium. Paint the stems green.

8 Use the large brush and more dark purple paint to fill in the the background.

9 Allow the paint to dry thoroughly.

10 Read the directions on the cans of spray paint. On one side of the bottom shelf, spray on several light layers of blue. Allow them to dry. Then spray on several layers of red until you achieve a color close to the purple background of the top shelf.

11 Place the shelves back in position in the cart with the painted sides on the underside.

DESIGNER: Diana Light

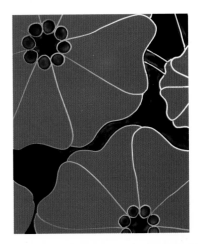

Contemporary Desk Accessories

Organize your desk with these clever techno-colored desk accessories for holding paper clips, pushpins, and rubber bands.

INSTRUCTIONS

1. Wash and dry the glass votive holders. Apply surface conditioner if recommended for use with your paints.

2. Squeeze out the paints onto your palette or plate. Load up one of the rectangular edges of one of your sponges with the colors.

3. Sponge on a rectangle that covers about one-third of one side of one of the holders, using the short, straight edge of your sponge to assist you in making a clean edge. The first coat will not be opaque. (Don't worry if the edges are slightly blurry.)

4. Use other paint colors to add a rectangle in the same fashion to each of the other three sides of both votives. Allow the paint to dry slightly, and apply a second coat of paint to the rectangles with the sponge.

5. Repeat steps 2 through 4 to add overlapping rectangles (both vertical and horizontal) in a variety of colors, allowing the forms to spill from one side to the next in a continuous design.

6. After you're satisfied with the overall design, sponge the lip of each of the votives with a different color.

7. Wipe off any excess paint on the lip with a moistened cotton swab. Allow the paint to dry thoroughly.

8. Cut out each of the design templates, and use transfer paper and a pencil to trace the outline of each of them onto one of the painted sides. (Think about the placement of the design in relationship to the overall pattern of your background.)

9. Dip the small, fine-tipped brush into a color of paint that contrasts with the background, and use it to outline the shapes. (If you make a mistake, you can remove the paint by lightly rubbing the surface with a moistened cotton swab.) Don't worry about making your lines perfect. These are supposed to be hand-painted pieces, not machine-painted!

10. Follow the paint manufacturer's instructions for either drying or baking the paint.

MATERIALS and TOOLS

- **3 square glass votive holders**
- **Mild detergent**
- **Surface conditioner (if recommended by the paint manufacturer)**
- **Opaque glass paints: white, black, bright blue, bright red, orange-yellow**
- **Artist's palette or old ceramic plate**
- **Wedge cosmetic sponges**
- **Cotton swabs**
- **Design templates (page 93)**
- **Scissors**
- **Transfer paper**
- **Pencil**
- **Small, fine-tipped brush**

DESIGNER: **Diana Light**

Wright-Inspired Mirror

Geometric lines and saturated color make this mirror classically modern with a nod to the designs of Frank Lloyd Wright.

INSTRUCTIONS

1 Clean the mirror with glass cleaner. Apply surface conditioner if recommended for use with your paint.

2 Tape together the pieces of the template to form a large pattern that fits on your mirror.

3 Slide transfer paper underneath the template, and trace the lines lightly onto the mirror's surface.

4 Lay pieces of self-adhesive lead line around the outside edge of the mirror first, and then lay out lead lines on the circular lines of the design. Use the craft knife to cut and piece the lines together.

5 Proceed to lay lead lines on the vertical lines and then the horizontal lines. Use the ruler to guide the lines as needed.

6 Dab a small amount of simulated leading on the spots where the lines connect. Allow the joints to dry.

7 Shake or stir the paints as instructed. Pour the paint straight from the bottle into the shaped spaces, following the color scheme in the finished photo. Use the fine-tipped brush to guide the paint into the corners. (The paint will shrink slightly when it dries, so be sure to get plenty of paint into the corners.) Pop any air bubbles with the straight pin while the paint is still wet.

8 Leave the piece in a horizontal position while it dries completely.

9 Follow the paint manufacturer's instructions for either drying or baking the paint.

MATERIALS and TOOLS

- Unframed rectangular mirror
- Spray glass cleaner
- Paper towels
- Surface conditioner (if recommended by the paint manufacturer)
- Design template (page 93)
- Masking tape
- Transfer paper
- Pencil
- 1/8-inch (3 mm) self-adhesive lead lines
- Ruler
- Craft knife
- Simulated liquid leading
- Opaque glass paints: yellow, red, blue, green, white
- Fine-tipped brush
- Straight pin

DESIGNER: **Diana Light**

Printed Leaf Table

Scattered leaf prints form a natural background for this outdoor or indoor glass-top table.

INSTRUCTIONS

1 Place the round glass top on the tabletop, and center it. Clean the glass with glass cleaner to remove dirt or smudges.

2 Apply surface conditioner to the front of the glass if recommended for use with your paint.

3 Squeeze out a portion of each of the glass paints on the palette or plate.

4 Place one of the dried leaf skeletons on top of a piece of old newspaper.

5 Load one of the sponges with bright green or dark green paint, and sponge the paint onto the leaf's surface. After you've completely covered the surface of the leaf, use a clean sponge to soak up the excess paint, allowing you to print a clearer impression of the leaf.

6 Pull the leaf gently by the tip away from the newspaper, and flip it over onto the table where you'd like to print it. Use the foam-tipped applicator brush to gently press it into place. (Try to keep the leaf from sliding.)

7 Go back over the leaf with the foam brush again, pressing down firmly on each part of the leaf to release the paint. Repeat this printing process with other leaves to add a pattern of scattered light and dark leaves to the table's surface.

8 Use a moistened cotton swab to clean up any mistakes that you make in the process of printing. Allow the paint to dry thoroughly.

9 If the base of your table is circular at the top, you can use it as a guide for sponging the large gold background circle. If not, cut out a large circle from the kraft paper, and tape it underneath the glass to use as a guide for sponging the circle.

10 Load up a clean cosmetic sponge with gold paint, and sponge the outer edge of the circle to establish its boundaries. (Don't worry about keeping the printed leaves within the boundaries of the circle; allow them to fall both inside and outside.)

11 Load up the natural sponge with gold paint, and sponge a light coat of paint inside the circle, covering any leaves within the area. Allow the paint to dry, and sponge another coat of light green paint behind the gold.

12 Allow the paint to dry for a day, then flip the glass top over so that the paint is on the underside of the table.

DESIGNER: **Diana Light**

MATERIALS *and* TOOLS

- **Large round glass tabletop with base**
- **Spray glass cleaner**
- **Paper towels**
- **Surface conditioner (if recommended by the paint manufacturer)**
- **Opaque air-dry glass paints: bright green, dark green, gold**
- **Artist's palette or old ceramic plate**
- **Dried leaf skeletons in several sizes (available at some craft or card-making stores)**
- **Old newspapers**
- **Wedge cosmetic sponges**
- **2-inch-wide (5.1 cm) foam-tipped applicator brush**
- **Cotton swabs**
- **Roll of brown kraft paper (optional)**
- **Masking tape (optional)**
- **Natural sponge**

Reverse-Painted Window

Transform an old window into art.

MATERIALS and TOOLS

- **Window frame with panes of glass (try asking for old windows at a business that installs new ones or look at architectural salvage or antique shops)**

- **Glass cleaner**

- **Paper towels**

- **Large sheets of white paper (such as sketch pad sheets)**

- **Masking tape**

- **Artist's palette or old ceramic plate**

- **Artist's acrylic paints or air-dry glass paints in colors of your choice**

- **Several brushes of various sizes**

- **Single-edged razor blade or craft knife**

INSTRUCTIONS

1 Clean the window on both sides thoroughly with glass cleaner (vinegar and water work well) to remove dirt and grime.

2 Do a sketch on sheets of large paper that will fit the window. (The design that you draw will be painted be reversed on the window.)

3 Tape the design facedown on the front of the window.

4 Turn the window over on it's face so that you can see the design behind the glass.

5 Squeeze out paints onto your palette or plate.

6 Paint the details and lines that outline the design first, keeping in mind that you're painting in reverse. Lift the window and look at the front to check the placement of your lines before continuing. If you make a mistake, scrape it away with the single-edged razor blade or craft knife. Allow the paint to dry slightly.

7 Add more foreground details to your painting, layering the paint behind the lines you've drawn. Continue to check your design on the front of the window as you progress, and allow the paint to dry if you don't want to blend the colors as you add layers.

8 Keep layering the paint until you've painted in the larger areas and the background.

9 Once you've completed the painting, paint one color over the entire back of the painting.

10 Follow the paint manufacturer's instructions for drying the paint.

DESIGNER: Claire Vohman

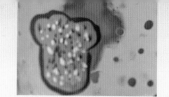

Cinnamon Toast Serving Set

This whimsical set sporting toast and toaster was created by the designer for her father, who loves his daily serving of cinnamon toast.

INSTRUCTIONS

① Wash and dry the glassware. Apply surface conditioner if recommended for use with your paint.

② Make duplicate copies of the two toast templates to transfer to the rim of the plate (smaller template) and the mug (larger template).

③ Tape the smaller toast templates to the bottom of the plate so that they are scattered around the rim.

④ Tape the larger templates to the inside of the mug in a random pattern.

⑤ Squeeze out small portions of the paints onto the artist's palette or plate. Use the small round brush to paint in the shapes of the toast on both the mug and plate with a mixture of ivory and burnt sienna. Allow the paint to dry.

⑥ Use the liner brush to outline the toast with burnt sienna.

⑦ To paint the toasters on the shaker, mix up a bit of ivory with the purple to lighten it slightly. Paint the sides of the toasters in regular purple, then paint the arch-shaped front in light purple. Allow the paint to dry.

⑧ Paint in two ivory highlight lines along the right side of the front of each of the toasters.

⑨ Complete the shaker by outlining the toasters and their cords in black. Add some light purple dots to the fronts of the toasters.

⑩ Follow the paint manufacturer's instructions for either drying or baking the paint.

MATERIALS *and* TOOLS

- **Glass plate and mug**
- **Glass cheese shaker**
- **Mild detergent**
- **Surface conditioner (if recommended by the paint manufacturer)**
- **Design templates (see page 93)**
- **Masking tape**
- **Artist's palette or old ceramic plate**
- **Opaque glass paints: ivory, burnt sienna, purple, black**
- **Small round brush**
- **Liner brush**

DESIGNER: Alice Disney Huelskamp

templates

Enlarge the following templates to a size that fits your particular piece or pieces.

Etched Wave Lamps,
page 34

Cut along
solid line

Sun Lantern,
page 38

Chinese Love Vase,
page 54

Stripes with Stars Bottles,
page 62

Note: Replicate as many times as needed to fit your vase.

Bamboo Vase,
page 50

Note: Replicate as many times as needed to fit your vase.

Faux Metallic Frame,
page 44

Note: Cut this template to a size that fits the border of your frame.

Retro Cookie Jar,
page 66

Contemporary Desk Accessories,
page 82

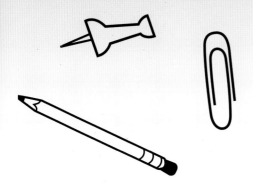

Silver Lining Cakestand,
page 68

Wright-Inspired Mirror,
page 84

Note: Enlarge this template in sections and then piece them together.

Cinnamon Toast Serving Set,
page 90

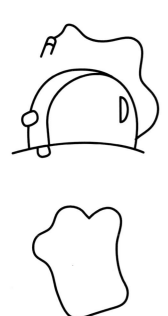

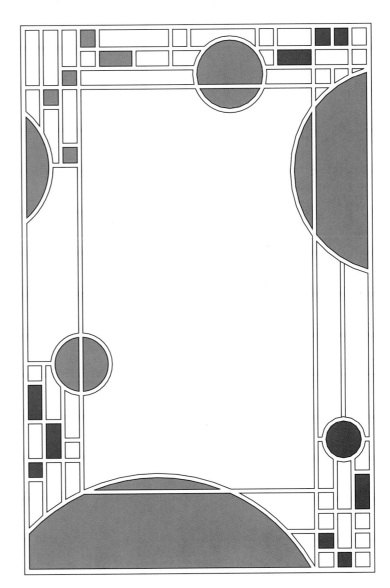

Flower-Power Roll Cart,
page 80

Catalina Fishbowl,
page 64

94

Main Contributing Designers

ALICE DISNEY HUELSKAMP (Pomona, California) learned to sew and paint as a child and has continued to explore her creative side. She earned a B.F.A. from Kansas State University and moved with her husband Clint to California after graduation. Today, Sara and Jacob, Alice's young children, keep her busy between designing and painting and are often an inspiration for her art work. Besides glass painting, she also enjoys watercolors, painting furniture, and painting for home decor.

DIANA LIGHT (Weaverville, North Carolina) is an accomplished artist and a frequent contributor to Lark Books. She holds a B.F.A. in Painting and Printmaking from the University of North Carolina at Greensboro. She now works in a variety of media, including oil and watercolor paints, paper, and photography. She does commissioned work and can be reached at dianalight@hotmail.com.

NICKY PAINTER (Menlo Park, California) lives and works in what she calls "one of the most diverse, creative and romantic areas in the world"—the San Francisco Bay Area. She notes that living in beautiful San Francisco provides her inspiration everywhere she turns. For years, Nicky painted everything she could get her hands on . . . furniture, pots, frames, and walls. She shifted her focus to glassware in 1997, and shortly afterwards resigned as a flight attendant to pursue her passion full-time. Nicky's work can be seen in wineries and gift shops throughout California and at nixnax.com.

Associate Contributing Designers

Katherine Aimone (Asheville, North Carolina) is an editor and writer for Lark Books. Most of her career prior to Lark Books has been in the museum field where she worked as a curator and director.

Tana L. H. Boerger (Washington, D.C.) is an artist and entrepreneur who, after twenty years of buying and selling companies, returned to her true passion, the creation of art. Currently, she combines business and art by creating designs that are licensed to manufacturers of home decor items.

Lynn B. Krucke (Summerville, South Carolina) is a mixed media artist whose interests include painting, stamping, collage, beads, fiber, fabric, and polymer clay. In addition to her design work, Lynn teaches a variety of mixed media classes at rubber stamp stores around the Southeast.

Brenda Star (DeLand, Florida) began her artistic work as an artist as a painter. Her painting has developed into many forms, including painting sculptural ceramics as well as commissioned portraits. Most recently, she has begun working experimentally with fused glass.

Luann Udell (Keene, New Hampshire) is a nationally-exhibited mixed media artist with a secret passion for carving her own stamps. Her fiber assemblages, embellished with her own handmade polymer clay artifacts, are inspired by the Ice Age cave paintings of Lascaux, France.

Claire Vohman (Tamassee, South Carolina) says that she has always doodled, drawn, and wanted to be an artist. After giving up her city lifestyle as a graphic designer, she now works out of her home in South Carolina, where her studio has a magnificent view of the mountains and a lake. She sells her painted windows (and many other items) at craft shows, galleries, and gift shops.

Index

Acknowledgments
thanks to:

Delta Technical Coatings for their donation of an array of air-dry glass paints that were used on many of the projects in this book. Thanks also for providing us with the name of one of our main contributing designers: Alice Disney Huelskamp.

Pebeo for providing glass paints to main contributing designer Diana Light for use on her projects.

Thanks to **all of the designers** who so patiently and quickly absorbed the concept of the book and created wonderful, inventive projects that complement one another.

Thanks to fellow editor **Marthe Le Van** for sharing the name of main contributing designer Nicky Painter.